ALIEN

Jemadari VI-Bee-Kil Kilele

To all victims of prejudice and stereotype

Copyright © 2022 by Jemadari VI-Bee-Kil Kilele.

ISBN 978-1-64133-892-9 (softcover)
ISBN 978-1-64133-893-6 (ebook)

All rights reserved. No part of this book may be reproduced or transmitted in any form or by any means, electronic or mechanical, including photocopying, recording, or by any information storage and retrieval system without express written permission from the author, except in the case of brief quotations embodied in critical reviews and certain other noncommercial uses permitted by copyright law.

The moral right of the author has been asserted in accordance with the Copyright, Designs and Patents act of…

This book is a work of fiction. Names, characters, places, and incidents are the product of the author's imagination or are used fictitiously. Any resemblance to actual locales, events, or persons, living or dead, is purely coincidental.

Printed in the United States of America.

Brilliant Books Literary
137 Forest Park Lane Thomasville
North Carolina 27360 USA

"I felt the urge to reassure him that I was like everyone else, just like everyone else."

Albert Camus, in **The Stranger**.

While asserting that this work is pure fiction, its author warns that any resemblance with one of the personages in this book would be a simple coincidence.

PROLOGUE

The "**Alien**" is a satirical look at the justice system in an African country where a foreign do-gooder is arrested on an obscure charge by a corrupt policeman, thrown in an overcrowded cell, and eventually released by the court.

At times the play is so realistic in its absurdity that one needs to remind oneself that it is an exaggerated parody of events and stereotypes and should bear no reference to the truth, although at times it seems to do so.

The final Act wherein justice is actually done completes the irony in that most persons remember with a great sense of injustice their day in court. Although witty at times, and cutting at others, this satire reminds one never to accept that all people think as one does oneself, that good deeds are often not only not rewarded but instead punished, and that in the larger scheme of things corrupt bureaucrats invariably get away with their actions.

On a serious note, however, the play also shows how indifference and lack of internal controls in a police station, and possibly any bureaucratic office for that matter, protects villains and fosters abuse of ordinary civilians.

Jerome Claasen BA (Hons)(UNISA)LLB(UCT)

LIST OF CHARACTERS

1. (male)Sergeant Bindzi
2. **Alien**
3. (female)Police Sergeant Pumza
4. (male)Constable Morobi
5. (male)Station Commander
6. (male)Sergeant Khumalo
7. (male)Constable Bantu
8. (male)Captain Lekota
9. (male)Staff Sergeant Moriri
10. (female)Police Inspector Lerato
11. Google: (inmate prisoner 1)
12. Skin Peel: (inmate prisoner 2)
13. Donovan: (inmate prisoner 3)
14. (Male) The Court Orderly
15. (Male) The Court Magistrate
16. Molema: Public Prosecutor
17. Bombela: The defence lawyer
18. Three persons from the public gallery
19. The public gallery.

ACT I

SCENE 1

[The Alien has picked up an ID book on the street pavement and honestly decides to bring it to the nearest Police Station. At the Police Station, people are seated on long wooden benches, waiting to be served while others are being received at different counters at the Oye Llevi police station. A police officer from behind the front desk calls him. Meanwhile, the last person to be served is just returning from the front desk. Few people are seated on a bench, waiting to be served on their turn]

Sergeant Bindzi:
Next. *[The Alien stands up from the bench and walks towards the counter] (In a commanding voice)* Yes, how can I help you?

Alien:
Good morning Sir.

Sergeant Bindzi:
I am not a Sir. I am a Sergeant. Can't you see? *[Pointing at his epaulet rank on the uniform shoulder]*

Alien:
Yes, Sir; I can see. You're a Sergeant; a police officer, sir.

Sergeant Bindzi:
Look, I told you I was not a "Sir". Do you hear me? Where did you learn your English?

Alien:
But Sir, I, I euh…

Sergeant Bindzi:
Look. Say, "Sergeant".

Alien:
[With a French accent] Sergeant, sergeant. *[The policeman starts laughing and invites his colleagues to join him. They ridicule the Alien with lengthy laughs and sarcastic comments].*

Sergeant Bindzi:
Look at this *Kwerekwere* who can't pronounce the noun "sergeant". *[A policewoman comments in her mother tongue]*

Sergeant Pumza:
These foreigners are so stupid. No matter how well you can try to help them out, but, they always give you hard time as they fail to communicate properly in English. Why do they come here? *[The Alien keeps standing there]*

Constable Morobi *[To the police woman]:*
Come on Serg...Do you expect everybody to speak English? I mean, to speak it perfectly?

Sergeant Pumza:
So what? Do you want to be his interpreter? Right. Go on. Please, do.

Constable Morobi:
Not really; Sergeant Pumza. I was just cautioning you on such stereotypical utterances.

Sergeant Pumza: Stereotype?

Constable Morobi:
I think we should not be attitudinal as regard languages. Being versed in English does not necessarily mean the other part who does not speak it fluently is not educated! How do you briskly label someone stupid, simply because his English is not as good as yours?

Sergeant Pumza:
Wena, what is your problem? Hein?

Constable Morobi:
There is none; Sergeant Pumza. I am sorry. But mark my words. Such utterances can one day land you in Shit Street. *[Then tries to exit]*

Sergeant Pumza:
To my plain knowledge, you cannot solve my problems if I am in trouble.

Constable Morobi:
Says who?

Sergeant Pumza:
We know you and we are used to you.

Constable Morobi:
Who are the "we"?

Sergeant Pumza:
Us women. Who else?

Sergeant Bindzi:
M'yeke [i.e. leave him]. *Wena* Morobi, stop quarrelling with a woman. Which type of man are you?

Constable Morobi:
Sergeant; I thought I was just advising her about the danger of some unprofessional attitude at the workplace. Nothing more.

Sergeant Pumza:
Unprofessional! *Usile wena.* Are you my manager here? My Station Commander?

Constable Morobi:
Frankly, that's not what I am aiming at. But...

Sergeant Pumza:
So, why are you interfering?

Constable Morobi:
I simply thought that a member of the police force should be non-sectarian because he or she was trained to protect and serve the public without discrimination.

Sergeant Bindzi:
Discrimination? Say that again.

Constable Morobi:
Discrimination. That is what I always sense at this station.

Sergeant Bindzi:
Wena Morobi, don't exaggerate *[Pointing finger at him]*.

Sergeant Pumza *[After staring at him]*: Who do you think you are?

Constable Morobi:
Nothing and nobody; if not a normal colleague of yours.

Sergeant Bindzi:
That's enough now. Please, guys, let's get to work *[Constable*

Morobi returns to working on his computer while Sergeant Pumza remains standing behind the counter, angered]

Alien:
[Who has been standing there so far] Yes, I am sorry sir.

Sergeant Bindzi:
[In mother tongue] You see. *Uyahlanya* this *Grigamba*. He does not understand anything at all. *[Returning to the Alien].* Yes, what can I do for you, stranger?

Alien:
[Touching his pocket] Yes sir, I have come to report to you that I picked this ID book up on the street; and thought of bringing it to this station so that you could find its probable owner.

Sergeant Pumza: *Utini?*

Sergeant Bindzi:
[To Sergeant Pumza] Just listen. *[To the Alien]* And then? What do you say you want me to do for you?

Alien:
I said, Sir, *[The policeman frowns his face]* I don't know the owner. So I preferred to bring it to you, you the authorities. *[He places the ID book on the desk]*

Sergeant Bindzi:
[Opening the Identity document] Hmm! Go on.

Alien:
Yes, sir. Now I withdraw myself?

Sergeant Bindzi:
"Withdraw"? Withdraw what? This is a police station. A house of law enforcement and protection, you see? We don't have a museum here to hoard archives; a bank or an ATM here to make some transactions. What is it that you said you want to withdraw?

Alien:
Eih, I mean…I just mean, I want to go.

Sergeant Bindzi *[Interrupting him]:*
To go, to go, to go where? Do you want a reward for this?
[He strongly throws the ID book on top of the desk]
You've stolen one national's identity book and (you) want this office to reward you for theft?

Sergeant Pumza:
Nkosi yame!

Alien:
Thank you, sir. I should now say bye-bye". *[Heading out]*

Sergeant Bindzi [*Still going through the ID book*]:
Please, don't go.

Alien:
Someone is waiting for me.

Sergeant Bindzi:
He knows you came to a police station; so he still will wait for you.

Alien:
Come on, man. What is this?

Sergeant Bindzi:
You thought it is a toilet where you get in and come out as you please? Neither is a church. Do you see?

Alien:
I am in a hurry sir; I have an appointment.

Sergeant Pumza:
Listen here papa; it has nothing to do with us.

Alien:
Why not? Anything wrong with you?

Sergeant Pumza:
Besides, can you show us your papers?

Alien:
Papers? Which papers?

Sergeant Pumza:
Your refugee or whichever legal documents that prove your status here in this country.

Alien:
My God; what a fuc…

Sergeant Pumza:
Hein!…An asylum seeker's document, something like that.

Alien:
Listen, officer. Do I really pose a security threat to this country by walking into your station?

Sergeant Pumza:
We don't exclude suspicion and presumption on people. It is all in the same pack as our job description.

Alien:
What? This is not an immigration office. Besides, why do you want me to walk around with my passport as if we were under constant curfew?

Sergeant Bindzi:
It's part of our job; man.

Alien:
I don't dispute that, but I think what I came here for was to report some matters. Why is it that you want even to take it further? I have got a copy of my passport. Is it what you want? *[Trying to pull it out of his pocket]*

Sergeant Pumza:
Not at all. We need the original.

Alien:
Original! *Mon Dieu! Mais, ces gens!!* But a photocopy is a genuine reflection of the original! And, it was certified by this office a couple of years ago!

Sergeant Pumza:
Ok. But, wait for a while *[She goes aside to whisper something into the ear of officer Bindzi]*

Alien *[Starting to go out]:*
So long, sir.

Sergeant Bindzi:
What? You're too impatient; stranger. It will not take a long time. Why are you so in a hurry?

Alien:
I am gone. *[Heading out]*

ALIEN

Sergeant Pumza:
[Shouting] Eyi wena; don't move out of there. We need your particulars. Perhaps the ID owner will need to contact you later. One never knows.

Alien:
For what? *[He returns to the counter, snatches the ID book from Bindzi's hand, then hardly throws it on the table]* I just picked up this fucken ID on the way to the grocery store, and then (I) decided to honestly bring it to you, perhaps you may find its owner. So where is the problem for you to continue harassing me, judging me as if I were a criminal?

Sergeant Bindzi:
Effectively, you are one. *[Turning towards Sergeant Pumza]* Just give me a charge sheet there.

Alien:
Mon Dieu. Qu'est-ce qu'il ya? (i.e. My God, what wrong have I done?)

Sergeant Bindzi:
What? Were you swearing at me? Are you swearing at me in your fucken mother tongue? *[Pointing a finger at him].*

Alien:
This is unbelievable! What's up?

Sergeant Bindzi:
Piece of shit. You can't just expect me to release you from these premises without your telling us in which circumstances you have found this ID book.

Alien:
But, but…but…

Sergeant Bindzi:
This is not a church where you expect people to believe in whatever you say.

Alien:
But…but… I wanted to…

Sergeant Bindzi:
[Touching the side of his head with his finger]

Alien:
You are taking it too far, man. Really for no apparent reason.

Sergeant Bindzi: *[After staring at him]*
You think you are clever and we are dunces? Stupid? Is it what you think we are? *Njandini!*

Alien:
But, but… *[Shaking].*

ALIEN

Sergeant Bindzi:
[Asking for handcuffs from his colleague in his mother tongue]: *Ngnike ama* handcuffs so that I can teach this fucken *Grigamba* a lesson. *Tsotsi.* *[Sergeant Pumza gives him the manacles]* Eh *wena;* these people; *Jeses;* these are those who are robbing us. *[He jumps over the counter and rushes to handcuff him.]*

Alien:
What wrong have I done? Heihn? What, what, what?

Sergeant Bindzi:
The wrong is that you are under arrest.

Alien:
For what?

Sergeant Bindzi:
Swearing and threatening me. You said I am not educated.

Alien:
When? When did I say that? And if ever I did say that, how can it be converted into an offence that gets one to be arrested?
[Sergeant Pumza starts laughing]

Sergeant Bindzi:
In your fucken mother tongue, you said to me "moonsieur"; keskilya", and so forth. That's terrible for me! Come here; give me your fucken hands.

Alien:
Mais, mais mon Dieu,... my God, what's happening? No one to help me around here? *[Comes in a 3rd policeman]*

Sergeant Khumalo:
Shut up, shut up you *Grigamba* *[Pushing him from behind]:* move, *puma*.

ACT I

SCENE 2

[The Alien is taken to another room where he is handcuffed and the steel chain is attached to a wall. He is seated on a chair. Comes in is sergeant Bindzi.]

Sergeant Bindzi: *[In a more cooperative tone through a mild attitude]* Today is Friday. You should know that there won't be any court open till Monday.

Alien:
So what?

Sergeant Bindzi:
I am going to lock you up. Your release will be subject to a fine.

Alien:
Do you mean bail?

Sergeant Bindzi:
Call it what you want, but that is how the judiciary system has conceived it this side of the world. It's a jackpot, you know? A money-making machine judiciary system.

Alien:
It looks funny, but at the same time strange.

Sergeant Bindzi:
I think you are an educated person. So, you should understand how it works. You see?

Alien:
Not really, but…

Sergeant Bindzi:
Justice belongs to those who have money.

Alien:
What about the poor? Aren't they human beings also?

Sergeant Bindzi *[Smiling]:*
There is no way out if you don't buy your liberty. You are out if you have money and in if you are poor or refuse to pay. It may be your present case here.

Alien:
I know, but I am not going to play that decadent game.

Sergeant Bindzi:
My friend; those who play it get away unnoticed; and still they are held in high esteem as good and honest citizens. So, it makes no difference, your refusal.

Alien:
It does.

Sergeant Bindzi: *[After a mocking stare at him]*
Well, as you like. But, you should think twice my man.

Alien:
I am innocently used to your cells. You should know that this will not be the first time I am being unjustly detained. And I always get out without paying a cent, you see?

Sergeant Bindzi: Meaning?

Alien:
As they don't find any crime with me, I just often get released.

Sergeant Bindzi:
We have no track record of that.

Alien:
Paying? Why?

Sergeant Bindzi:
This time, you will. You'll pay some charge fees, my friend.

Alien *[Starring at him]*:
Tell me; what wrong have I done to you for you to put me in these shameful shackles?

Sergeant Bindzi:
You should know, those are shackles of justice. You are a suspect. You stole my country man's identity book and pretended to play the innocent. We know you.

Alien:
What would I have gained had I lied to you?

Sergeant Bindzi:
You know yourself. But, that's not my business.

Alien:
It is. Certainly, it is your business.

Sergeant Bindzi: *[After staring at him]*
Mine is to arrest people like you; who mock on host country's laws and expect to get out scot-free. That's my business. Do you see?

Alien:
I did not do anything wrong. I am not a trespasser. So… what's your motivation?

Sergeant Bindzi:
Probably you attacked him and stole money from him. Now for you to get rid of his ID book, you come to report its loss to our station.

Alien:
That's an odious distortion; nothing else. You're just fabricating things.

Sergeant Bindzi: *[Staring at him]*
We are used to your tactics. You see, you *kwere kweres are* unpredictable. You come here empty-handed. The next thing, you become tycoons with our money. It's a mystery.

Alien:
That's a fallacy. Unfounded allegations, if not mythomania. We work for all that we have. What's your problem?

Sergeant Bindzi:
You have brought fraud into our country, prostitution, STDs, drug pushing, and all sorts of societal ills. So, we are prepared to deal with you. No stone will be left unturned. It's just a matter of time.

Alien:
This is not fair. *[The policeman sternly stares at him again as he prepares to take down his details]*

Sergeant Bindzi:
What's your name?

Alien:
Ever since I am here; you should have started from there instead of bullying me.

Sergeant Bindzi:
Am I bullying you? Am I? What is your fucken name? I am just doing my job.
[At that moment, the station commander passes by]

Station Commander:
Anything wrong here, gentlemen?

Alien:
Thanks for coming in sir. I am just being…

Sergeant Bindzi:
Shut up. Who asks you to fucken speak? *[Slapping him]* Yes, Sir *[Turning to the Station Commander and saluting him]*.

Station Commander:
What's happening here, Sergeant Bindzi?

Sergeant Bindzi:
Just doing my job sir, as I was taught.

Station commander:
Hmm. So why is this person cuffed?

Sergeant Bindzi:
Chief, this chap, I mean, euh…he refused to co-operate; and he nearly went berserk during the interrogating process.

Station commander:
Is that so?

Sergeant Bindzi:
I beg your pardon.

Station Commander:
Did he resist the interrogation?

Alien:
No. I…

Sergeant Bindzi:
Shut up. Yes, he did. Yes, he did. So, regrettably, I had no other alternative apart from subduing him in this manner, Chief.

Station Commander:
It looks inhuman, though. It recalls the olden days of Apartheid; you know?

Sergeant Bindzi: Do you think so?

Station Commander:
I do. Did he at all raise his hand on you?

Sergeant Bindzi:
Pardon me, sir.

Station Commander:
Was he physically violent towards you?

Sergeant Bindzi:
Bbb…but Chief, a blatant insult is more painful than a slap on the face.

Alien:
Uh! But, sir *[To the Station Commander]*, I did not insult him. I simply came to rep…

Sergeant Bindzi:
Shut up. Didn't I order you to shut it? You must respect my Station Commander. *[Sternly looking at the Alien while pointing at the Station Commander]*. The more you talk the bigger the indictment if you don't know. Watch out.

Alien:
This is unthinkable. How can someone just go ballistic for no apparent reason!

Station Commander:
You, over there *[To the Alien]*, cool down.

Sergeant Bindzi *[To the Alien]:*
Your constitutional freedom and rights will only be guaranteed on the one condition that you obey my instructions and allow me to do my job.

Station Commander:
That's right. Go ahead.

Sergeant Bindzi: *[Twisting the Alien's ear]*
Since you have been here, I am trying to help you, and...

Station Commander:
Take it, easy sergeant. Can I get that charge sheet you're holding?

Sergeant Bindzi:
Sir, *[A bit reluctant]* I was in the process of taking his statement when you walked in.

Station Commander:
And then? What prevented you from doing it?

Sergeant Bindzi:
But the man is just a difficult character and should be lectured in one way or another.

Station Commander:
Still, I need the charge sheet; sergeant.

Sergeant Bindzi:
You'll get the docket later, Chief. *[The station commander looks irritated, but keeps quiet.]*

Alien:
Bbbbbut…I didn't…

Station commander:
OK. Cool down, gentleman. *[Turning to Sergeant Bindzi]* You, carry on with the statement in the meantime. I wish to receive it on my table as soon as you complete it. *Right?* *[Exit]*

Sergeant Bindzi:
Ok, Chief. *[Slamming the door, mimicking the Station Commander; then snarls at the Alien]:*
So, you stupid *Kalanga*, you thought I was going to mince my words in front of the Station Commander? Or else he was going to release you?

Alien:
That's not what I intended. You're simply a bloody twister.

Sergeant Bindzi:
Repeat what you've just said. *[Kicking him]* Repeat it. A bloody what? *[Then he slaps him on the jaw. The Alien stands up and catches him by the collar resulting in the policeman defending*

himself; then each and every one shouts at the other]. Your bloody mother. Son of a bitch.

Alien:
It's better to be a thief and corrupt like you. You're lucky because I am one hand handcuffed. I would have shown you what I am made of. Useless framer.
[Comes in rushing two police officers: a male and a female]

Sergeant Pumza:
Sergeant, sergeant, what's wrong?

Alien: *[To sergeant Bindzi]*
You think I can be afraid of you because you carry a gun? Put it away and you'll forget your way out of here.
[Mr. Alien keeps on grumbling, struggling to get out of the grip of the shackles]

Sergeant Khumalo *[Entering]*:
Sergeant, *eh wena Bindzi, please stop this ugly fight in here. If he fails to co- operate, we'd better hurl him into* the van and drive him to a bigger cell in Brow Hill Police Station. Jesus! Why waste time with this bastard. We've got a lot to do, you know? We are on a night shift patrol downtown, man. You could have finished this for a long time. Don't give any dam time to bastards.

Alien:
I am not a bastard. My parents are still alive and happily married to date. You must withdraw that. Instead, you are the ones acting superbly like bastards.

Sergeant Bindzi [*To Sergeant Pumza*]:
What? Inspector, did you hear that?

Sergeant Bindzi:
[*Turning back and pulling his gun out of its holster, then points it to the head of the Alien*]: You dare say that again, you fucken bastard; I'll blow your fucken skull out. [*He holds him by the neck; then other two police officers intervene*]

Sergeant Pumza & Khumalo:
No, no, no sergeant. We'd better lock him up here until morning.

Sergeant Bindzi:
Unfortunately, we don't have cells to accommodate suspects here. We'd better take him to Brow Hill police Station wherein his skin will be peeled off by our cell-resident guys.

Sergeant Pumza:
But how? Till now, you haven't jolted down any of his particulars yet. How would we be allowed to lock a clandestine up whose identity remains unknown? It's unprocedural.

Sergeant Khumalo:
Vamus, let us leave this matter to sergeant Bindzi himself. He is a big boy. He knows how he will get his statement,

even under duress. It's allowed. There are many ways to kill a cat as they say.

Sergeant Pumza:
Only, it's taking time; and the cat is resisting dying.

Sergeant Khumalo:
Had it been me, I would have disposed of him in my only way.

Sergeant Pumza: How?

Sergeant Khumalo:
Like this *[He makes a nasty neck slitting gesture]*.

Sergeant Pumza:
Woah!

Sergeant Khumalo: *[On the way out]*
These people are giving us a tough time at this station. More stringent measures should be introduced; specifically for them. They shouldn't benefit from much freedom and rights as the country's citizens do!

Sergeant Pumza:
Besides, they were not here when we suffered for our democracy. Where were they when our forefathers were fighting Apartheid? Hm! Just a bunch of democracy

profiteers. A cohort of beggars and human rights whistle-blowers.

Sergeant Khumalo:
Anyway. Sergeant; we are waiting for you outside. Please, don't delay. *[Exit both Sergeants Pumza and Khumalo. Sergeant Bindzi nods]*

ACT I

SCENE 3

[Still in the temporary detention cell. Bindzi is left with the Alien]

Sergeant Bindzi:
You may sleep in an icy place my *broo if* you don't co-operate.

Alien:
[Staring at him as he is still manacled] Cooperate in what?

Sergeant Bindzi:
I told you earlier on, my man.

Alien:
What wrong have I done to you? Are you normal?

Sergeant Bindzi:
Have you diagnosed any abnormality in me?

Alien:
But….

Sergeant Bindzi:
Are you a psychiatrist to…?

Alien:
My God! What is this?

Sergeant Bindzi:
Watch out, my man. Things may turn sour if you don't stop your stubbornness here.

Alien:
You must know that; the wearing of this uniform does not bestow on you the authority to control my destiny, nor should you think that, because I am not of your country you have the license to ill-treat me. You're just as human as I am. And that's that.

Sergeant Bindzi:
Wena Grigamba; this is my country. And, you have no right to teach me anything; you know?

Alien:
Naturally, everyone comes from a certain country. Do you forget that? I didn't fall from the sky like a stone.

Sergeant Bindzi:
I know that pretty well.

Alien: So?

Sergeant Bindzi:
But this one is my country. It's my asset and you can't challenge me for it.

Alien:
Well, I don't dispute that. And I am not here for that. I am ordering you to set me free. Now. That's all.

Sergeant Bindzi:
My colleagues are outside waiting for me. I should be joining them by now.

Alien:
So, who is preventing you from doing that? First of all, let me go, and then you'll go too. Can't you see that I am helping you to solve a useless problem you have stupidly created?
[Sergeant Bindzi lights up a cigarette, smokes some part and kneels down to puff its smoke out on to the Alien's face]

Sergeant Bindzi:
[After staring at him] What's your name and surname?

Alien:
Alien. I told you that earlier on.

Sergeant Bindzi:
Is that your name? *[He jolts it on the paper after a long stare at him]*

Alien:
Yes, it is. What more do you want?

Sergeant Bindzi: Surname?

Alien:
Human Being *[The policeman gets angry and starts stomping the floor with his feet]*

Sergeant Bindzi:
Are you kidding me?

Alien:
Not really. But you've been kidding with my life ever since I am unjustly cuffed here.

Sergeant Bindzi:
[He leaves the paper and pen on the table and goes out for a while]

Alien *[Left alone]:*
My natural status is not much different from the citizens of neither this host country nor any other. We all are

temporary creatures here on earth. We all are passers-by; aliens. To some extent, short and fragile is our sojourn on earth. Authority, glory, wealth, health, fame, and you name it, do not make anybody holder of eternal earthly citizenship or nationality. A human being is a stillborn creature. While living, we just ignore that we are ambulant corpses. We walk while being dead. So, why all this arrogance?

Sergeant Bindzi:
[Returning in and throwing the cigarette butt onto the Alien]

Alien *[After staring at him]*:
Are you now satisfied? You feel great. Don't you?

Sergeant Bindzi *[Sitting face to face with him]*:
Tell me; why do you foreigners behave like new *conquistadors in our* country?

Alien:
Woah! Is that the unique impression you pick out of us?

Sergeant Bindzi:
It's displayed in all your mannerisms.

Alien:
Do you mean?

Sergeant Bindzi:
The way you talk, walk, dress and even look at us. You seem to be looking everyone down. We are nothing for you, yet we host you.

Alien:
That is a calumny or else misinterpretation of an erroneous and generalized psychological judgment.

Sergeant Bindzi:
Do you think so?

Alien:
Why do you overload your mind with such baseless fear?

Sergeant Bindzi *[Standing up]*:
Fear? Do you think we are afraid of you?

Alien:
Afraid? Why should you? Certainly, this is your country.

Sergeant Bindzi:
At least and at last, you recognize it.

Alien:
It makes no difference. We're still the same race, same people; and human beings.

Sergeant Bindzi:
There is a difference. I don't want to highlight it now; for you are under arrest.

Alien:
Why are you preaching this *cainism philosophy* to me? I am just your brother man. And I did not come here for this nonsense.

Sergeant Bindzi: Nonsense?

Alien:
Yes; nonsense and *cainism.* Nothing else.

Sergeant Bindzi:
Cainism? Am I the biblical Cain?

Alien:
To some extent, yes; you are.
Something of a Black supremacist among Blacks.

Sergeant Bindzi:
But I am not jealous of you! Cain was jealous of his brother Abel.
Not me. What do you have in the first place for me to be jealous of you?

Alien:
Besides jealousy, there is that hatred that you are piercing me with like a spear. It is in your words, your utterances, your look, your stereotype, and prejudice; yet I and still am your brother man.

Sergeant Bindzi:
Hmm! Brother man? And you said we are the same people?

Alien:
Yeah, same people. Yes, we are the same.

Sergeant Bindzi:
Eish, I doubt. Look; the majority of you people are pitch black than us.

Alien:
That's true, it's the colour of the continent; it's our common identity, and it makes no difference…We are one.

Sergeant Bindzi:
Tell me; why are you here?

Alien:
Because our DNA is the same. Both you and I share the same melanin.

Sergeant Bindzi:
You go too scientific now. Melanin? *[He keeps quiet for a long time, then looks up to the Alien again.]* You come here because you have nothing in your countries. Isn't it? Mine is a paradise. Will you deny that?

Alien:
Many races and many individuals from all over the world flock to what you call your country; why do you single me out of the multitude? Why? *[Sergeant Bindzi walks aside and gives his back to the Alien. Then looks at him degradingly by turning his head.]* Why? Am I the softest target? *[Sergeant Bindzi looks disturbed.]* You are afraid of those whose pigmentation differs from ours. I mean yours and mine. Isn't it?
[Sergeant Bindzi keeps quiet for a long while again; turns around and around; then smiles a bit; then lays his hand on the Alien's shoulder.]

Sergeant Bindzi:
Do you take me for a monster? Do you think I wear a white mask?

Alien:
That we know of sure. You do. Nonetheless, we all are still the same people and same race. *[Sergeant Bindzi keeps quiet for a long while; turns around and around, then bends down low to speak to Mr. Alien]*

Sergeant Bindzi:
Same people? Let not the colour of the skin mislead you. For the mentality, the living standard and so forth are not the same.

Alien:
Don't minimize me. I am warning you.

Sergeant Bindzi [*After staring at him*]:
You are a joke. Look, Alien. Talk like a man.

Alien:
Do you mean?

Sergeant Bindzi:
I think you are adult enough, and surely (are) able to understand what I mean. Use your mind and, you'll talk.

Alien:
I am a man and, I do not need to revisit my mother's womb and be born a man for a second time.

Sergeant Bindzi:
Men have got their manhood language when they face a problem. Consequently, to solve it they use men's language.
Men's language? I would be thankful if you could teach me that language. I hope it's not late, my Sergeant.

Sergeant Bindzi:
Certainly, it's not late yet. One's got to be a man sometimes to do things; you know?

Alien:
Regrettably, I am astonished to learn for the first time that I am not a man, only in this police station!

Sergeant Bindzi:
Physically yes, as a human being, you are a man, but fail to talk men's business language. *[Enter another police officer]*

Sergeant Khumalo:
Uh! Sergeant! You're still here? The engines are started and you risk being marked absent for tonight's patrol. What's going on in here?

Sergeant Bindzi: *[Smiling]*
Serg. Just a routine job. Look, this gentleman refuses to facilitate my things in my work. I would have joined you ever since had he supplied details needed for this affidavit. He thinks he's clever.

Sergeant Khumalo:
Well, like any other foreigner. They are all like that; these people from Africa. But in the end, everything always ends in our hands. We are in control. *[Shouting at the Alien] This is our country.*

Sergeant Bindzi:
Tell him, Sergeant, tell him. He sounds disconnected from reality.

Sergeant Khumalo:
All right. *[To Bindzi]: Inspector,* would you please leave him with me?

Sergeant Bindzi:
Why? Why would you like to kneel down in front of this bastard? Let us throw him into the van and drop him in Brow Hill cell so that he could taste the icy floor and breathe the stench of stinking blankets. *[He stands up and leaves both the pen and papers on the table, then exits].*

Sergeant Khumalo:
[Sitting on the chair and trying to persuade the Alien]: Listen here my brother; this man is dangerous. Very bad I tell you; and, I am afraid he may harm you.

Alien:
What for?

Sergeant Khumalo:
Hm! Well!
I want to know the reason for his planning to harm me. Why don't you get informed about the reason for my being chained here? Am I a criminal? What is it that he told you that I have done?

Sergeant Khumalo:
No, my brother. Not at all. But, once in this situation you are a suspect, not really a criminal as such, but sort of…

Alien:
Of what? What have I done in the first place? What? Hein, tell me?

Sergeant Khumalo:
I wouldn't know for sure. For, I was not there when all this rubbish started?

Alien:
Rubbish! Do you call injustice "rubbish"?

Sergeant Khumalo:
Calm. Please cool down my *broo*.

Alien:
You horrendously arrest people without any cause; you frame them and dare call that rubbish? Is it what you were taught during your training time? *[The sergeant, surprisingly stares at him]*

Sergeant Khumalo:
Listen. I am not here to arrest you nor to judge you. Rather, I want to help. You should know, I can't take over his job. Everyone here in this police station has cases to handle under his power.

Alien:
Funny! It's just weird, all this approach.

Sergeant Khumalo:
[Pause]. Listen, why can't you just take a shortcut and get released instead of pulling this tug of war too far?

Alien:
Do you mean?

Sergeant Khumalo:
[Starring at him]: Brother, you're failing to read his mind? I think the inspector needs a Coke, and that's all.

Alien:
A Coke? Where will I get a Coke when I am shackled? Is he Coke-thirsty? Is it for a Coke that I have been detained ever since?

Sergeant Khumalo:
Well, that is what I may guess. He's a colleague of mine, and I know sometimes how he deals when in need. I am afraid, I can't help.

Sergeant Khumalo:
No, no, no, no; my brother. Cool down. You can. Of course, you can. Only that you refuse to comprehend.

Alien:
But how?

Sergeant Khumalo:
Look how you are. A gentleman like you; so well dressed, trendy, with all these glittering pieces of jewellery on... You can't continue pulling things to this extent.

Alien:
I don't think I am different from you.

Sergeant Khumalo:
You are. Of course, you are, my brother. You see, I am just a uniformed man.

Alien:
Meaning?

Sergeant Khumalo:
My life is a synonym for poverty; shady existence, etc....

Alien:
Sorry for that; but whatever stuff I wear, is simply decorations to attract ladies and give myself a respectable status out there.

Sergeant Khumalo:
For a man, that's absolutely perfect. Nonetheless, there is still something feasible prior to that, my brother.

Alien:
Something? What is that something?

Sergeant Khumalo:
Listen here, my brother, we earn money to solve problems. Isn't it?

Alien:
Talk. I am listening.

Sergeant Khumalo:
Fine. And now, you are in and have a problem.

Alien:
So what is it that you want? It's absurd.

Sergeant Khumalo:
But why are you hardening your heart? You are a man. I know. But…

Sergeant Khumalo:
He needs this… *[Rubbing his thumb and five fingers to imply money]*

Alien:
What! Do you need money? Money from me? *Mon Dieu! I can't do* that. Even if I had it on me, I would never attempt to bribe him. Other people can. Not me.
[Enter Sergeant Bindzi]

Bindzi *[Storming from the back]*:
Then, we're taking you with us. Serg…Help me, but don't loosen the handcuffs. *[To the Alien] Stupid.* Stingy. You have wasted our time for nothing; *[They drag him away]* yet we are trying and willing to help you out. Idiot.

Sergeant Khumalo:
[Pushing him]: Puma. Let's go.

ACT II

SCENE 1

[The Alien has been transported to the Brow Hill police station owing to the lack of detention cells at Oye Llevi Police Station. Together with two police officers who have helped to transport him, they are in front of the counter. There are three police officers behind the counter. The Alien is handcuffed and resists being seated by force. Sergeant Bindzi finally pushes him to sit down on the bench]

Sergeant Bindzi:
[Pushing the Alien on the visitor's bench] Sit there, and don't you fucken make any move. Do you understand?
[Then proceeds to drop the file on the counter, then talks to an-on duty officer]. As usual. *Mfo wetu,* this guy is too stubborn. So we wish to teach him a lesson so that he can no longer joke with us.

Constable Bantu *[Behind the counter; reading through the file]*: Hm! What is his name?

Sergeant Bindzi:
My brother. I am tired of this man. All along, he's been refusing to supply details about his true identity. He calls himself Alien, Human Being, and so forth and so on. All in all, his speech is a supreme contradiction of terms...

Captain Lekota:
So, how do you bring us here a suspect whose identity remains a mystery to you?

Sergeant Bindzi:
You have a mouth. So, get him to speak to you. As for me, I am done. Utterly disturbed by his negative boldness.

Constable Bantu:
Ok. He will open up to me if we torture him; this Mr. Alien or Human Being, whatever his name.

Sergeant Bindzi:
But, can someone be called like that?

Constable Bantu:
What do you think? That's not strange.

Sergeant Bindzi:
How? And why?

Constable Bantu:
What is a name, after all, Sergeant? Isn't it a word that helps identify someone or something, and which was given to you by your parents? And which they believed in?

Captain Lekota [*Coming from behind Constable Bantu*]: Say that again.

Constable Bantu [*To sergeant Bindzi*]:
Well, go through many dockets [*Pointing at a shelf*] there and you will discover what you call funny names.

Captain Lekota:
I will. Thanks. [*Smiling*]

Constable Bantu
You find people whose names are "Lovemore, Open, Learnmore, Studymore, Backdoor, Tragedy, Charisma, Respect Fish, Gunford, Forward, December Job, Kaffir Job, Soccer, Computer; Professor, Counselor, Queen, Jealousy, Mouton, Cabinet, and you name it. What can you do? It is their names?
[*Other officers start laughing*]

Alien:
Thanks, officer for vindicating me.

Sergeant Bindzi:
Shut up, *Grigamba*. [*Then approaches captain Lekota*]
Come on captain [*Whispering some words onto his ear*]

ALIEN

Captain Lekota: *[Nodding]*
Now you're talking my language; Serg…

Sergeant Bindzi: Now you see?

Captain Lekota:
Ok. That's alright. Hm! *[To the Alien]* Gentleman, come forward. This side.

Alien:
[Rising up from the bench and advancing towards the counter] Here I am; in flesh and bones.

Captain Lekota:
That's all right. Please, put down here all the valuables that you have. You should not worry. We'll keep them safely for you until you are released or sentenced; perhaps.

Alien:
All my all is valuable. What do you mean?

Captain Lekota:
Money, cell phones, belt, pieces of jewellery, and the likes. You're not allowed to enter with anything inside the cell. Not even your shoelaces or necktie.

Alien:
Why not?

Constable Bantu:
Look, that's what the law says. If you want to challenge that, wait until you are released. Some other days, perhaps. But not today.
[Constable Bantu loosens the handcuffs from one hand while having them on the other.]

Alien *[Starts taking them off, one by one]*:
These are my assets. What more do you want? *[Pointing at his wrist watch and gold chain]*
I have no trust in envious people like you.

Constable Bantu:
Don't worry. The station has got a safe. Surely all your assets will be recorded on a document, a copy of which will be handed over to you after you have signed it.

Alien:
Ok. But, how can I do it? I am still handcuffed. Can't you see?

Sergeant Bindzi:
Ok, they will remove the handcuffs. *[To Captain Lekota] I see you tomorrow morning. But, don't forget our* deal.
[One constable completely removes the cuffs from the Alien's hands. Mr. Alien continues putting his items on the desk, one after another. Lekota comes from behind the counter in order to handcuff Alien again.]

Constable Bantu:
Please, hang on a bit until we lock him up.

Captain Lekota:
[To the Alien]
Hurry up! Take off your shoes too. This is not your home. Remember, you are under arrest. Your rights are however recognized but limited. So, watch out chief. Things may turn sour and tough for you if you don't change.

Alien:
Must I take off my clothes as well?

Constable Bantu:
Who asked you to do that?

Alien:
But clothes are valuables too!

Constable Bantu:
Do what you are instructed to do and don't exaggerate. Otherwise, we'll lock you in for a week before you see the sun. Hurry up. *[Having been standing around, Lekota comes from behind the counter and handcuffed him again]*

Captain Lekota: *[Holding a file and a pen]*
What's your name?

Alien:
I am Mandangu *[The policeman jolts it down in a file]*

Captain Lekota:
Ma what? *[Starring at him]*

Alien:
Mandangu.

Captain Lekota:
OK. Surname?

Alien:
Olusegun Mama Nayo.

Captain Lekota: *[He looks at him with amazement]*
That's a kilometric surname!

Alien:
You're not here to question my surname? What do you…

Sergeant Bindzi *[Returning]*:
Shut up! *Grigamba*. *Bandit* from a poor country where there are no tomatoes.

Alien:
Mostly you *[Pointing at Bindzi]*, you'll know me when I come out of here.

Sergeant Bindzi:
Aah! *Suka*. You are nothing.

Constable Bantu:
[Instructing another policeman] We are used to criminals' threats in here. Take him. Take him away from here now.

Staff Sergeant Moriri:
Wena, asihambe. *[Pushing him ahead of him, then stops for a while.]*

Captain Lekota:
Please, Serg…Hold him up there first, or else bring him back again here to the bench.

ACT II

SCENE 2

[Still at the Brow Hill Police Station]

Constable Bantu:
[Aside. To Sergeant Bindzi] Before I read the docket, Serg, tell me; what has he really done, this man before we throw him in the cell. I see you are angry with him.

Sergeant Bindzi:
Well, that man is a thief. He is a Nigerian or a *Kalanga, something like that; Eish! Really, angazi. He was caught stealing an ID document of a South African citizen. Someone saw him and came to alert us.*

Constable Bantu:
And where is the complainant, well, the…your informer?

Sergeant Bindzi:
You'll see him in court when he will come to testify. He was so busy that he didn't want to come along with us and then shortly, he left for his other businesses. But surely, this bastard deserves some punishment.

Constable Bantu:
That's what these people do. They remove people's photos from within the ID book or passport, replace them with theirs and start getting credits and loans from the banks, yet we the natives who fought for our freedom, sweat to get those loans and house bonds. Bank would require collaterals, this and that before approving your loan application.

Constable Lekota:
Say that again. Oh yeah. I still remember a couple of years ago how I suffered for my house bond…

Constable Bantu:
Tell you what? Congolese fraudsters call that scam of documents falsification, *Mbangula, Ngunda [Police officers start laughing]. No, Inspector, thank you. But something must be done against these aliens' scourge in this country. Really our ancestral land must be cleansed.*

Sergeant Bindzi: Absolutely, yes.

Captain Lekota:
The long arms of the law will redress the situation. *Don't* worry. *[In a low voice] But,* you said he's a Nigerian?

Sergeant Bindzi:
I think so. Because, he speaks French, oh no no; I think English. Do they speak English in Nigeria?

Captain Lekota:
No, Sergeant Bindzi; only *Gananians* and *Angolians* do. But Congolians speak French.

Sergeant Bindzi:
Are you sure?

Captain Lekota:
100%. Nigerians are those who display big biceps in public, unashamedly leaving their chests bare and also peddling drugs on the streets. But, as you may know; they are good at soccer.

Staff Sergeant Moriri:
Most Nigerians bleach their faces with cosmetic chemicals and end up looking like whites, but soon when they don't have money they return to their charcoal pigmentation.
[Collective laughter from surrounding officers]

Captain Lekota:
Is it?

Staff Sergeant Moriri:
Yes! Don't you watch their movies?

ALIEN

All their ladies are yellow…ripe unpeeled banana. Their thighs, arms, and faces are peeled off like ripe bananas, while their hands and fingers are burned like a blacksmith. *[Collective laughter from surrounding officers. Moriri continues.]*
One would hardly question if these people are Black Africans?

Captain Lekota:
Hybrids, or perhaps they are Euro-Africans.

Staff Sergeant Moriri: Who knows?

Constable Bantu:
That's why they are called "Aliens". *[More laughter from the police officers].*
For, with such a mixed skin complexion, they seem not to belong to this planet. *[More laughter from all the police officers]*
They are multi-coloured. *[More laughter]* …That means, they have several skin colours in one body. *[More laughter]*

Captain Lekota:
They must have a lot of cash to uphold such a de-pigmentation process.

Captain Bindzi:
What are they pursuing in denaturalizing their skin complexion like that?

Captain Lekota:
Well, 'should ask Michael Jackson who is their inspirer. He remains a guinea-pig of plastic surgery; a victim of his own success, money, fame and glory. Not really proud of what God made of him.

Staff Sergeant Moriri:
So are all the Nigerians, Congolese, Cameroonians, and the likes. The bleaching trend is even invading our country now. Just look at some of our women now, and what they're doing once they come into contact with these people from overseas.

Sergeant Bantu:
Especially those of our ladies who are of dark skin complexion like these aliens, they too have started bleaching their body.

Captain Lekota:
It's deplorable. They are imitating more particularly these Congolese and Nigerian nationals.

Captain Lekota:
Yeah. Above all, these Congolese and Nigerians. They talk loudly; with a funny accent. They say "*my moni, my moni, my brada, my brada…* [*To the Alien*] My brada, are you also a Nigerian?

Alien:
As you like. But I am just a human like you. *[Laughter and amazement from the police officers]*

Staff Sergeant Moriri:
Sorry, my *brada*. I didn't mean to hurt you. *[Back to his colleagues]* But they have a lot of money those crooks.

Constable Bantu:
Money?

Staff Sergeant Moriri:
Oh yeah. They do. I have a friend, a Nigerian friend who always takes me out and treats me well. In fact, some of them are good; I should tell you.

Constable Bantu:
Do not generalize. Some of them may still be as poor as we are. Like this one here. *[Pointing at the Alien] He pretended that he had nothing on him.*

Staff sergeant Moriri:
Oh yeah; man. Did you say Nigerians and Congolese?

Constable Bantu:
Yes, I did.

Staff sergeant Moriri:
These two categories of Africans like wearing suits, man. Expensive suits; even when the weather is hot. *[More laughter]*

Captain Lekota:
They are chic. But, they run corner street churches everywhere now like *spaza shops. They are pastors.... all of them. Pastors in suits...*

Sergeant Bindzi:
But, who told them that God of Israel cannot receive their prayers unless they are dressed in suits?

Staff Sergeant Moriri:
Perhaps God of Israel holds a fashion show every Sunday. Who knows? The reason why they go to their churches to compete in fashion.

Sergeant Bindzi:
I think God of Israel wears suits too. *[Laughter]*

Staff Sergeant Moriri: I really think so.

Sergeant Bindzi:
If you want to release him, ask for something. You know. These *Kwerekwere do* have solidarity. His fellowmen wouldn't hesitate to run for his rescue by popping out a few dollars when they learn that he's in jail. *[Entering P.I. Lerato]*

Constable Bantu:
Watch out! Your colleague is coming in.

Police Inspector Lerato:
Bindzi: *[In IsiZulu] Asambe. We are late, the patrol chief wants to talk to you on the radio. 't's important, it sounds like.*

Sergeant Bindzi:
Wena sisi, I will not eat him. We're looking for kids' beans. Chiefs are well paid. We're not, *sisi. Do* you understand?

P.I. Lerato:
Bins! You mean…your children do not have dust bins in their bedrooms?

Sergeant Bindzi:
Are you with me or not, Lerato?

P.I. Lerato:
Oh! Certainly, I am. Did you say bins? Bins? Didn't you?

Sergeant Bindzi:
No, no, no, no. You're not in my scope. *[Aside]:* If I were talking about sex to you, all your senses would have been aroused.

P.I. Lerato:
Eh batho!

Sergeant Bindzi:
Can't you understand when I say beans? Beans: b, e, a, n and s. I mean this…hein? T*shelete wena. Not* where we put garbage. *Comprendo?*

P.I. Lerato:
[Amazed] What? You mean,

Sergeant Bindzi:
Keep off. You're wasting my time. Our banks and farms are these suspects. Some of us have bought cars and houses in these connections; why does not your patrol chief allow me to do what he's been doing? Chiefs have got fleets of cars in their yards; bought thanks to extortion. But for us, we do not. So why don't you want me to do the same?

P.I. Lerato:
Please, answer the radio *[Presenting the walkie-talkie]*

Sergeant Bindzi:
Tell him, he is in the toilette. Do you understand? I am in the toilette. *Hamba [Pushing her extended hand.]* (*To the officers*). The *Grigamba* has money. So, he can pay for his release and we shall strike that case out of the role. Don't forget about me, gents. We will declare the docket was stolen; *Finito [Exit]*

Constable Bantu:
Don't worry. Eh *wena Lekota*, let us take him to the cell, man.

Captain Lekota:
[Coming out of the corner. To the Alien]: Chief, follow me.

Alien:
Where to?

Captain Lekota:
You've been under arrest ever since. Don't you know that? Your constitutional rights are recognized and guaranteed, but you shouldn't push me to lose my temper.

Alien:
I will not move from here. Kill me if you want.

Captain Lekota:
[Dragging him from the bench]: This way, this way, you stupid. Fucken *Kalanga*. Follow this way. *[Kicking him]*

Alien:
[Resisting] *Aren't* you the ones who are supposed to protect citizens of this country?

Constable Bantu:
Sure. We are. And then?

Alien:
Yet you turn now into callous torturers. Are both guns and uniforms empowering you to bully people?

Captain Lekota:
Shut up. *Grigamba.*

Alien:
You are violating my rights. Are both guns and uniforms empowering you to bully people?

Constable Bantu [*Joining in*]:
Sjambok him so that he can learn a local lesson. This is South Africa, hein! You're not this country's citizen. You're an asylum seeker. An alien. So, zip it up.

Alien:
So what? Is it a sin to be a foreigner in another country?

Constable Bantu:
You don't deserve the same treatment as a local citizen.

Alien:
I never said I was a local citizen. Surely, one day I may return to my country.

Constable Bantu:
Good riddance. That will be fine. It is the greatest wish of all of us in this country. For, our country is too stuffed by you as the number keeps on rising to majority like swarms of locusts.

Alien:
I doubt. You are stretching it too far, officer.

Captain Lekota:
Really, we are squeezed. No space is left for us the indigenous people. From rural to urban areas; you are everywhere. Spreading all over like the tentacles of an octopus. It is a slow-motion occupation.

Alien:
I doubt if it is one. *[Constable Bantu wickedly stares at him]* Will my return to my country bring material happiness to you? Will it add any value on to your life?

Constable Bantu:
It will, to some extent; yes, it will.

Alien:
I will go back to my country. Let us hope you will be promoted to higher rank into the police force.

Constable Bantu:
And if you refuse to return to your fucken country…, besides, to some extent, you are an *apatride as they say in French. A stateless citizen.*

Alien:
I am not. I belong to a country. Please, stop insulting me and do what you came to do instead of indulging in futile rhetoric. *[Alien tries to stand up from the bench]*

Constable Bantu:
Why do you leave your fucken and hungry countries to come here? Fuck. Piece of shit. N*zokotubula, wena.* Don't jock with me *[He slaps him on the jaw].*

Alien:
[After staring at him] The conduct of you men and women who are hired to protect the public is a case in point, and needs to…

Constable Bantu:
Shut up. There is nothing you can teach us. Go back to your fucken and hungry country where you can hold such lecture sessions. Not here. This is *Mzansi, man; euh! Fo sho. The city of gold, not of beggars. Siyasebenza here, man.*

Alien:
It's astonishing how you consider yourselves as a law unto yourselves. Once those uniforms are dropped off, you're not different from us. Why are you so arrogant, rude, and think you are above the law?

Captain Lekota:
Tomorrow, you'll talk another language, my man. *Lindela is* waiting for you. We will deport you. And soon, you'll miss our country. Many deportees always end up returning here, jumping our borders illegally like mice.

ALIEN

Staff Sergeant Moriri:
Ehin! They always sneak in like mice; these people. Too many of them are undocumented. Consequently, they must be rounded up and swiftly deported to their countries.

Alien:
Returning to my country is not a ruling of execution. I am still able to recycle my life there as well as anywhere in the world, you know?

Constable Bantu:
So why don't you just go home and leave our country?

Alien:
I fit everywhere. Immigrating here does not mean running from starvation in my country. There are many underlying reasons. I am working here; paying my tax and contributing to your country's economy. Which is my economy too. I am not a ruffian.

Constable Bantu:
Good citizens do not steal; *wena. You are* confused.

Alien:
I stole nobody's asset. I did steal nothing at all. What's my offense? Can you prove it?

Staff Sergeant Moriri:
The affidavit reflects a theft case of someone's ID. Truly, you are a *tsotsi*.

Alien:
Bullshit. You don't know what you're talking about. Did you read the xenophobic report made by your colleague? If at all he did make it.

Staff Sergeant Moriri:
You mean?

Alien:
Well, I could see him even struggling to write. Can he write? Can he spell a word? His fingers were shivering to hold the ball pen!

Staff Sergeant Moriri:
You are mad. He was not promoted to the rank of sergeant for nothing. Surely he has some dose of literacy. What do you think?

Alien:
Besides, I didn't sign it. So whatever accusation it is, it does not hold any water.

Constable Bantu:
Ahead of big events like the soccer world cup, it is the police's duty to clean up the streets of bad elements,

bad citizens like you who want to usurp the country's citizenship and create a hub of criminality.

Alien:
Man, you don't understand the difference between a national and a citizen of a country. All of us humans, always tend to improve our lives in one way or another by crossing one's country's border.

Captain Lekota:
Eh bana! He is talking. What a strange face of courage!

Alien:
I am not asking to be a South African of origin, and I was not dragged to this stinky hole to discuss the notion of citizenship or nationality with you. Do you see?

Staff Sergeant Moriri:
So what? Constable Bantu? He's just angered.

Sergeant Bindzi: Yes.

Staff Sergeant Moriri:
Throw him into the cell before he vomits more insanities onto our faces. What type of a man is this? He's not afraid of us.

Alien:
As long as I live in a certain place on earth and abide by the country's laws, I too am a citizen of that country.

Staff Sergeant Moriri:
Such citizenship should be granted to you by the host country.

Alien:
That I know of. But…I am in the process of being naturalized. Are you satisfied with that?

Captain Lekota:
None knows on which visa did you enter our country.

Alien:
You are digging deeper now, my man. I am a legal immigrant here.

Captain Lekota:
Do you often renew your immigrant status?

Alien:
You've got to read the papers that you hold.

Captain Lekota:
Despite that, you are not wanted here. Do you understand that?

Alien:
I can't be told.

Constable Bantu: *[He stares at him]*
You can talk, eihn!

Alien:
Well, you make me talk. Read Genesis in the Bible. Also, read Exodus 22:20 [23:9, Leviticus 19:34, etc....Jews crossed the borders, leaving Israel for Egypt, into Africa; looking for greener pasture. Such is not different from my case. I mean our case.

Staff Sergeant Moriri:
Given all that rhetoric, what prevents you from returning to your...

Alien:
There are many underlying reasons as I said.

Captain Lekota:
Enough now. Take him away *[He is pushed ahead in the alleyway towards the cell, then exits.]*

ACT II

SCENE 3

[Still at Brow Hill police station. An incoming telephone rings]

Constable Bantu:
Brow Hill Police Station, officer Bantu speaking. Can I help you? *[listening] Ok,* ok, yes. The suspect is already in the cell and yes, yes. Ok. Like some other suspects who are here; their cases will be heard in court only on Monday hm. Ok, bye.
[Returning in is officer Lekota]

Captain Lekota:
Done?

Constable Bantu:
Hundred percent. He's kicked in, and I have asked our boys to deal with him in there. He will learn an unforgettable lesson after a full night of beating inside the prison.

Captain Lekota:
Very good. He really will learn his better lessons there. He deserves it.

Staff Sergeant Moriri:
It will be an unforgettable lesson for him after a full night of beating by those guys in there…

Constable Bantu:
True… he will learn that sometimes the rules of the game end up changing.

Captain Lekota:
He is stubborn that guy. He seems to know too much. So the only way is to get rid of him in one way or another.

Constable Bantu:
He thought he was at home here. He forgot he was at a school of life; *Mzansi*.

P.I. Lerato:
Wena Lekota. Please, we shouldn't go to that extent.

Captain Lekota:
Wena sisi; where is your problem?

P.I. Lerato:
Ehn! *Hahle wena. I* am just advising you. *Akiri freedom* of speech is enshrined in our Constitution?

Captain Lekota:
Certainly.

P.I. Lerato:
So, why should you envisage eliminating someone physically, just for a simple exchange of words?

Captain Lekota:
[Pointing at her]: I am not astonished by such sudden intervention. It is you ladies who are betraying the nation. You.

P.I. Lerato:
Betraying who? And how?

Captain Lekota:
Most of you go out with these drug peddlers and money launderers.

P.I. Lerato:
Eh! Hang on a bit. What are you saying?

Captain Lekota:
Here, you are an officer; out there, you are no one but everybody's property; mostly with these aliens.

P.I. Lerato:
And then? Where is your problem? Do you want to cage me? To cage me like a bird? We are free to do what we chose and want. What does it have to do with you?

Captain Lekota:
They are nothing, but microbes that come to infest and infect our society.

P.I.Lerato:
Wena, Lekota. You are wrong. They are men like you.

Captain Lekota:
Like who?

P.I.Lerato:
If they are more caring and loving than you are; what more do you think a woman can do?

Captain Lekota:
So, you can't live on your own? Anyway, I am not surprised. I knew you would argue that way.

P.I.Lerato:
And so! Universally, which woman elects to suffer in her life? Can you show me one that you know of?

Captain Lekota:
You always dream of being taken care of?

P.I. Lerato:
Why not? It is our nature. You can't change it. Can you show me one woman that wants to suffer? Simply because she loves you or you subdue her because of your masochism? Customs and traditions?

Captain Lekota *[After staring at her]*:
So you blow with the wind?

P.I. Lerato:
They are not winds. Many of them are good and responsible husbands. They don't beat us; they don't kill us nor abandon their offspring as you do. A practice that is one of your heritage.

Captain Lekota:
[Getting angry]: *Usile wena*

P.I. Lerato:
Yourself. For you to support your kids, you must necessarily be dragged to a maintenance court. And,..

Captain Lekota:
All is due to your promiscuity. Isn't it? You remain unsatisfied; too curious as you like exploring new lands and reaching the bottom line of everything.

P.I. Lerato:
Gosh! What about you? Aren't you the first to abuse us? Unfaithful men. Greedy and selfish. How many girlfriends of yours do we see coming here to…?

Constable Bantu:
Please, stop that ugly talk here. That's one's private life.
[He intervenes to separate them and keeps on talking to both in a low voice]

P.I. Lerato:
So? He is the one who started. I am not married to a foreigner. But, if it happens that I got one who treats me well and loves me, I will not hesitate to engage myself in such a relationship. And I don't need your permission to do that. Where is your problem? A woman is like a fish. She goes where water flows.

Captain Lekota:
Look at it here. Listen to that garbage.

P.I. Lerato:
…and I don't need your permission to do that. Where is your problem? A woman is like a fish. Shall I repeat? She goes where water flows. Do you want to rule like a coq over hens in a farm? Alone?

Captain Lekota:
Wena, umakhosha wena.

P.I. Lerato:
I am not. Your wife is. That's an unfit slur.

Captain Lekota:
[Jumping on the lady's neck]: *Ngizokudubula, wena sisi,* watch out *[Touching his gun holster].*

P.I. Lerato:
Dare, dare it if you are a real man; *[She also touches her gun holster]* Satan. *[Two police officers intervene to separate them]* Half-man. You are a masked criminal who ignores his crimes in this police station. You're known. Only colleagues fear to spill the beans.

Captain Lekota:
Ah! *Fusek.*

Constable Bantu:
Sisi Lerato; it's enough.

Staff Sergeant Moriri:
Please, please, you two, stop this.

P.I. Lerato:
If you dare lay your hand on my body, I will open your wardrobe, and people will discover your skeletons in there.

Constable Bantu:
Ok, Ok, sister; cool down. Please, cool down.

Staff Sergeant Moriri:
Well, this is not a parliament where you women go vocally ballistic to show how much equal you are to us.

P.I. Lerato:
It is women's right to defend themselves against masochism, men's patriotic instinct as they think that all powers are divinely bestowed to them.

Captain Lekota:
Wena Lerato. I am not your Nigerian boyfriend.

P.I. Lerato:
You can't even be one. I have a man. And I mean a man. You can't match him. *[Captain Lekota stares at her, then leaves to the back room.]*

ACT III

SCENE 1

[This scene opens inside the temporary prison cell wherein the Alien is detained with other suspects, all awaiting to appear in court on Monday. It is still Friday night. A policeman opens the cell gate and pushes him in. Mr. Alien is welcomed by a thunderous uproar of inmates. Some are seated on sponges while others are lying on them. They are strangely dressed]

Captain Lekota:
[Pushing him in] Go in there, *pa nse, pa nse, wena* stupid *Amanyasa*. *[The Alien sits down and tries to identify those around him]*. Sit down. *Inja*. *[A group of other inmates is lying on the sponges, smoking drugs and other sorts of cigarettes, and they are drinking alcohol too.]* Hey! Look at these bandits. They are drinking! *[He leans down to confiscate some bottles of beer and starts drinking too. Soon after, the police officer slams the door and leaves.]*

Google: *[To Alien]*
Welcome to GP, the **Gangsters' Paradise,** my *broo*.

Alien:
Thanks, who are you, if I may ask.

Google:
The caretaker of all newcomers. I will treat you well here, provided you buy me a cigarette as the right of admission to our club.

Alien:
I don't smoke nor do I wish to belong to any club. I am here as a detainee. Arrested for no reason.

Skin Peel:
We all are detainees, broo. But we don't complain. You'll get used to these four walls and heavy concrete roof above your head my *broo. Just sit down and relax.*

Alien:
Thanks. Which cigarette were you requiring from me, you? *[Pointing at Google].*

Google:
Any way. A cigarette is a cigarette, no matter the name or brand.

Alien:
Unfortunately, I don't smoke. Besides, how do I call you? I am Olusegun Mama Nayo.

Google:
Do you need my name?

Alien: Sure.

Google:
[He starts laughing] Olusegun. It sounds Nigerian.

Alien:
I am not one. I am just an African as you are.

Skin Peel:
That's good. We don't say you are a European. Listen, we're not ridiculing you. I am **Skin Peel,** and that's a simple identification. You see that man there; his name is **Google. That means he is Good for Girls.**

Alien:
Well, I am not a girl. Are you myopic?

Skin Peel:
Neither am I, and moreover, I am not myopic. In all actual facts, we all come here with our innate genders; once inside this hole, our human nature mutates from male to female or vice versa. Sort of animalism; you see? It sounds strange!

Google:
There is nothing strange about that. Besides, tonight, you'll be my wife. 'you understand?

Alien:
Your what? Are you mad? *[Everybody laughs] Listen* here, I am not a homosexual. We don't do that in my country.

Skin Peel:
Certainly not. He is not gay.

Alien:
Watch out. I am not a homosexual.

Skin Peel:
There is always a beginning. I mean the first beginning to everything.

Google:
This is not your country. Here, our Constitution allows us to do all we want. It is borderless freedom.

Alien:
What? Do you mean a sort of *libertinage*?

Google:
Eihn! Something like that. Unrestricted freedom. Thus, don't import your sick African cultural dictatorship here. Do you understand?

Alien:
You are praiseworthy. But, time will tell one day.

Google:
Garbage.

Alien:
Take it easy, man. I don't mean to minimize you.

Google:
Shut up. Here, we are born free. A born free generation. My *broo. You… you people from Africa, forever are* chained in your political and cultural ignorance, my *broo. Backward* mentalities are not permitted in here. Here, it's a land of the free. Democracy. Do you see?

Alien:
Do you think so?

Google:
I don't think. I live it. We are living freedom. Eating freedom and smoking freedom.
That's mental sickness. Nothing else.

Google:
Please, take. *[Handing over to him a pack of cocaine]*

Alien:
What is that?

Google:
Here is a sweet tablet; a sort of elixir to arouse you, buddy.

ALIEN

Alien:
Then do it on yourself. I can't be your sexual guinea pig to release your hibernated libido.

Donovan:
Try it. Just for a while.

Alien:
In my country, when one is in that need, one searches for a woman and vice-versa. Not what you're dreaming of doing to me.

Donovan:
He is right, Google. You are talking about constitutional freedom; so he is also free to choose. You can't force him.

Donovan:
Shut up, Skin Peel! It has nothing to do with you, brother. This one is mine.

Alien:
If you dare make a move towards me, you'll be a dead man. Do you hear me?
[Standing up] Dead; and your chapter on earth will be closed.

Google:
I'd wish to see that. *[Then starts laughing]*

Donovan:
Google, I think he is right. Africans yes, we all are, but some evil practices are abject in some societies. Remember…

Donovan:
Skin Peel; I say fuck off. Who asks you to intervene? Get sleep under your stinky and hole-riddled blanket *[throwing it onto him]*. And you *[to Alien]*, as you question my instructions, you will sleep naked, shivering on this icy floor without a blanket. *[He produces a revolver and points it to Mr. Alien]*

Alien:
[He stares at him] I don't care, and I am not scared. You know, only abnormal people find it comfortable to sleep inside a prison cell.

Google:
And you think I am abnormal?
Well, the reason why you are carrying a firearm everywhere.

Google:
Even so-called ''normal people'' own guns. Where is your problem?

Alien:
Normal people dedicate their time to thinking; reasoning, initiating, organizing, managing, and mainly working.

How do you enjoy this incarcerating status here? Being fed hard crumbs of bread and putrid porridge?

Donovan:
Many talk like you, but we end up bedding them in here. We'll see.

Alien:
I can't shoulder such African cultural predation. It is a shame if we Africans start bartering our cultural values with destructive democratic anti-values.

Donovan:
What do you call anti-values? Eihn! Look at this hooligan! How do you label satisfaction of one's desire as "destructive"?

Alien:
I am not there.

Donovan:
You are here already, my *broo; and* we'll ask you to taste it with us this night. It just takes one to be initiated. And hoop! One gets rolling.

Alien:
Forget about me. *[Noise of walking boots is heard near the door]*

Skin Peel:

Please, stop it. Stop discussing you bastards. *[In a low voice]* The police are here *[The door is slam-banged]*

Staff Sergeant Moriri:

[Beaming a torchlight on the cell inmates] Stop discussing you bastards. It's too late and your bloody noise is disturbing the premises. One more noise and I will soak all of you with a bucket of icy water. Eh *bathu*! They have been drinking beer *[He collects a few bottles and leaves, slamming the door behind him.]*

ACT III

SCENE 2

[In the magistrate court. It's 9 o'clock a.m. Suspects arrive handcuffed and are soon seated on a front-row bench. Enter the Magistrate. Inside the court are the Public Prosecutor, Alien, and his defense attorney as well as the public gallery]

Court Orderly:
The court, rise.

Magistrate:
[Ordering the audience with his hand] Thank you. Please, you may be seated.

Public Prosecutor Molema:
[With an open file on the pulpit, the PP leans to greet the magistrate, then turns to greet the audience too]. In this court of Brow Hill, the matter to be heard on this first-order in the case of Mr. Alien and the state. Dear audience, Mr. Alien

Olusegun Mama Nayo; sorry. *[Turning to the suspect]* Am I pronouncing well your name, sir?

Alien:
No, don't worry. All are fine.

Public Prosecutor Molema:
Thank you. I was saying, Mr. Mama Nayo Olusegun, is, according to the statement contained in this docket, taken *verbatim by* the court, accused of stealing a South African National's Identity Document last Friday, after assaulting him and robbing him of his money. A sum estimated to be Rands 500. After leaving his victim stranded on the street, he ran away with the booty. Soon later, he then turned into a Good Samaritan by bringing the ID of his victim to the Oye Llevi Police station, all this in a gesture of a good citizen. It's there, after tight interrogation, and establishing his guilt that sergeant Bindzi decided to arrest him.

Alien:
Lies; lies. You're lying. It's not true.

Bombela: *[Approaching Mr. Alien]*
Please, cool down. Chill out. Leave the defense to me. Please, keep your seat. *[Addressing the Public Prosecutor]* Your honour, I am attorney Bombela, defending Mr. Alien.

Magistrate:
That's right.

Bombela:
My client, to my best knowledge, is completely innocent in this entire saga. Let me just say, this court has no case against my client.

Magistrate:
We'd like to know how and why.

Bombela:
Your worship and dear audience; Mr. Alien, my client, has been framed by some police officers, most especially the one my honorable colleague Molema claims to have interrogated him. A certain Bindzi, Bonza or Bindza. My apology, your worship. In fact, and in contradiction to his statement, suffer to get informed that, my client has resisted bribery temptation; and I pre-empt, after this session, he will be hailed as a hero in defeating these outgrowing malpractices in our modern society.

Magistrate:
Can you perhaps elaborate more on that for our absolute enlightenment?

Bombela:
Your worship, our country is on a brink of an administrative collapse. There is a rampant plague in our midst. Corruption and bribery have penetrated all our societal fabric. This plague must be curbed without delay, your worship.

Magistrate:
Which one?

Bombela:
Your worship, an officer who is corrupt and who aims at extorting money from an individual in exchange for his freedom should not be kept in our police force.

Magistrate:
Please, go on Bombela.

Bombela:
My client, having refused to bribe officer Bindzi, is dragged here for nothing. In addition, my client has been abused by his captors who heaped him with xenophobic insults and other kinds of degrading utterances, unacceptable for a man of dignity and a world's class citizen like my client.

Magistrate:
Go ahead.

Bombela:
My client is of such a high caliber and should enjoy his rights as a human being like you and me *in lieu of* being humiliated to this extent!

Magistrate:
Officer Bindzi, what do you have to say against the attorney's allegations?

Sergeant Bindzi:
[Standing up and advancing towards the microphone]:
Your worship; as a security officer of my state police force, I duly deem that I have played my role of protecting the public. Mr. Alien is insolent, and violent and has refused to cooperate with me.

Magistrate:
How?

Sergeant Bindzi:
He refused to answer my questions and insulted me that I was not as educated as he is. *[Alien is agitated and attempts to intervene]*

Magistrate:
Does it really suffice to arrest him and have him spend 48 hours in a cell?

Sergeant Bindzi:
Well, what more can I say? I was offended. Yeah, just offended; you know?

Magistrate:
So you took it personally?

Sergeant Bindzi *[With eyes cast down]:*
To some extent, yes; but…

Magistrate:
Officer Bindzi, did you read him his constitutional rights before locking him up?

Sergeant Bindzi:
Yes, yes, Yes, I did, your honour; yes, I did.

Alien *[Slightly agitated]:*
That's not true. You abused me, you and a couple of your colleagues. You told me that I am not a South African citizen, so I should "fuck off". Furthermore, you asked me "to talk like a m

Magistrate:
Meaning?

Alien:
Your worship; interpreting his insisting request, I may deduce it in money demanding. He and his colleagues required bribe from me if I needed to be released and avoid being locked up. And that, I refused.

ALIEN

Bombela:
[Rising his hand and asking for the floor]

agistrate:
Yes, proceed; Bombela.

Bombela:
The manner in which my client was chained, primarily handcuffed, forced to sit down while dressed in a suit, your honour, was dehumanizing. Totally degrading.

Magistrate:
I see, and I remain empathetic to him.

Bombela:
Little do you know is the treatment he received inside the cell, your worship; where he had to fight hostility by resisting rape from an enraged horde of homosexuals who threatened to sodomize him.

Magistrate:
Sorry.

Bombela:
Such treatment meted out against a man of rare qualities like Mr. Alien, whose real name is Olusegun Mama Nayo; is nothing but xenophobic, discriminatory, uncivilized

behavior. Moreover, any officer who continues to indulge in corruption malpractices should be combated with the strongest dose of energy and dismissed from the police force.

Magistrate:
Officer Bindzi.

Sergeant Bindzi:
Your worship; I have done my job, and I have no regret whatsoever.

Magistrate *[Starring at Bindzi]:*
Bindzi?

Sergeant Bindzi *[A bit nervous and unruly. To the Magistrate]:*
You, you call it allegations, but these are degrading and unfounded accusations against me. I serve this country.

Magistrate:
That's obvious.

Sergeant Bindzi:
Lawyers are there to look for their money.

Magistrate:
And then?

Sergeant Bindzi:
So they defend even lies and criminals. He *[Pointing at Bombela]* was not there when all this happened!

Magistrate:
I don't buy that, Sergeant Bindzi. Please, I am warning you to be in line with my questions and respect the contention of the plaintiff and his attorney…

Sergeant Bindzi:
I promise to comply; your honour. I will. But.

Magistrate:
Mr. Alien, would you briefly tell the court how much officer Bindzi asked from you? Any witness?

Alien:
Your worship, I would lie to quote an amount. However, he asked for money in exchange with my freedom. And that has astonished me. For, surprisingly, I did not realize which offense I committed in bringing to the police station a lost identity document *[Magistrate nodding]*. *How my good deed turned into an offence, that I certainly can't tell, your honour? It's a nightmare for me?*

Bombela:
A nightmare indeed; yes, it really is. Our police force must get rid of these rotten fruits and pot-beliefs who are tarnishing the values of our Constitution.

Person 1 *[From within the Public Gallery]:*
Police management must ensure that these rotten potatoes are taken out of the system.

Court Orderly:
Silence in court. You are an attendant and not a suspect nor an attorney. Not even a witness.

Person 2 *[From within the Public Gallery]:*
These policemen are reversing the constitutional gains our country has so far hardly achieved in improving relations between the public and the police force.

Court Orderly:
Silence!

Person 3 *[From within the Public gallery]:*
We are all victims of these officially uniform-clad officers, but masked thieves who terrorize us in the city.

Court Orderly:
Shut up. I said zip it up. And I don't want to repeat myself.

Magistrate *[Standing up]:*
Indeed, the state should cut these weeds; it should prune these bad leaves and branches from the trees so that everybody can enjoy freedom and liberty in this country.

Public Gallery:
Yeah; that's it, that's it. *[Clapping hands]*

Magistrate:
We should display humanism towards those citizens of our world who choose to come and live in our country as their second country.

Public Gallery:
Of course, we should. *[Round of applause again]*

Magistrate:
The law should be the same for everyone as stipulated in the Declaration of the Rights of Man, in France in 1789. No matter where one comes from.

Public Gallery *[Pointing at officer Bindzi]:*
Yes. Lock him up too. Lock him up. *[Round of applause again]*

Court Orderly:
Silence, please. You'll be kicked out of this court if you don't stop interfering.

Magistrate:
Thanks. Ladies and gentlemen; after cross-examination, I have not sniffed any wrong doing from this man. With the power that the state has vested in me, I order his immediate release after these court proceedings. *This is a judiciary flop.* *[A big applause from the audience]* *Mr or rather*

officer Bindzi will be disciplined internally, according to the rules and regulations of our police force.
[With his hand, Sergeant Bindzi dismisses the Magistrate's statement]

Public gallery:
Yeah!

Magistrate:
Our modern society has no room for xenophobic officers, liars and framers, who violate human rights, and intimidate community members whose taxes pay us.

Public Gallery:
Yeah!

Magistrate:
We all are aliens on earth as we end up dying one day, leaving all what we have.

Public Gallery:
[Big audience applause]

Magistrate:
Intimidation, harassment, corruption, bribery, extortion of money and all those evils which dent the fabric of our society will be exposed and eradicated as we all aspire for a more democratic, inclusive and universalized world.

Public Gallery:
Yeah!

Magistrate:
This is the only way we will sustain our diversity; not by reviving the old demon of division and discrimination. We have defeated Apartheid and colonialism. We are the survivors of the Cold War. We are, we are...Ladies and gentlemen; corruption, bribery and xenophobia are not high mountains for us to climb.

Public Gallery:
Yeah!

Magistrate:
Ladies and gentlemen, we will conquer those evils. Yes, we will. Look, it's not a matter of obligation, but it's humanity. It's what you do as a human being *vis à vis another human being. That's all. We should not be arrogant or thinking we defeated Apartheid and colonialism ourselves only. In fact, it was a world synergy.*

Public Gallery:
That's it. Tell him, tell it to the money-mongers. The beans-collectors and Coke-drinkers.

Sergeant Bindzi:
[In a low voice] You all are fools. All. Small heads.

Magistrate:
Many of those you discriminate against have done wonderful things in our country. Their contribution has benefitted some of us. This proves that an 'immigrant is not only that person who flees his country with his luggage on the head for a safer place, but it is the one who runs with his head to make a better place for all."
[The Public Prosecutor and the Magistrate stands up to a thunderous applause of the audience and leaves the stage. And so does the Magistrate]

Court Orderly:
Court, rise.

The End

GLOSSARY

Kwere-kwere: a foreigner [*a common slang/a derogatory word in South African indigenous languages*]

Wena: you [*in IsiZulu & IsiXhosa and siSotho*] Eyi, wena:

M'yeke: leave him/her [*in IsiZulu & IsiXhosa*]

Usile wena: You are naughty [*in IsiZulu & IsiXhosa*]

Uyahlanya: you are crazy [*in IsiZulu*]

Grigamba: a foreigner [*a common slang word in South African indigenous languages*]

Utini: What? [*In IsiZulu & IsiXhosa*]

Nkosi ame: My God! [*in IsiZulu & IsiXhosa*] Mon Dieu!

Mais: My God! But! [*in French*]

Eyi, wena: eh, you! [*In IsiZulu*]

Mon Dieu. Qu'est-ce qu'il y a: My God. What is happening [*French*]

Njandini: You, dog [Isi*Zulu*]

Nginike ama handcuffs: give me the handcuffs [IsiZu*ulu*]

Tsotsi: a criminal [*a common slang word in South African indigenous languages*]

Mais, mais, mon Dieu: but, but, my God! [French]

Kalanga: a foreigner [*in common slang in South African indigenous languages*] or else, especially (a tribe in) from Zimbabwe or Mozambique.

Mfo wetu: My brother [Isi*zulu* & *IsiXhosa*]

Angazi: I don't know [IsiZulu]

Mbangula: A Congolese slang for "falsified document"

Ngunda: A Congolese slang for "refugee paper"

Sisi: sister

Jeses: Jesus [in Afrikaans] **Gananians:** Ghanaians **Angolians:** Angolans

Tshelete, wena: money, you [*siSotho* & *siTswana*]

Comprendo: understand! [Spanish]

Hamba: Go [Isi*Zulu* & *IsiXhosa*] **Finito:** Finish [Spanish/Italian] Sjjambok: to slash or beat someone with a stick [in Afrikaans] **Fuseck:** Go away [in Afrikaans]

Nzokudubula, wena: I'll shoot you [Isi*zulu*] Siyasebenza: we are working [Isi*zulu*]

Lindela: A deportation camp at the outskirt of Johannesburg.

Eh bana!: Eh people! [*Sisoto & sistwana*]

Hahle, wena: relax [IsiZulu]

Ankiri: Isn't it? [*siSotgho & Sisetwana*]

Usile wena: You are naughty [IsiZulu] **Ngizokudubula:** I will shoot you [IsiZulu] **Pansi:** down, sit down [IsiZulu]

Inja: dog [IsiZulu]

Akiri: Isn't it? [In

Broo: a colloquial word for "brother"

Amanyasa: an immigrant from Malawi or Zambia. It is a derogatory word to mean, foreigner, especially from Malawi.

Mzansi: a slang for "South Africa"

Si ya sebenza: We are working [in IsiZulu] **Fo sho: for sure Angazi: I** don't know [IsiZulu of Isixhosa] Vamus: let's go [Spanish] **Jesses: Jesus [Afrikaans]**

Wena, umakhosha: You are a bitch! [IsiZulu]

Puma: Go, leave [IsiZulu]

STDs: Sexually Transmited Diseases. **Wena, asihambe:** you, go. [IsiZulu] **Brada:** brother

Eh batho: eh, people.

Conquistador:

Mfo wetu: our brother. Suka!

Wena, asihambe: You, let us go.

Mbangula: A Congolese slang to mean falsified document. Ngunda: also, a Congolese slang to mean falsified document. **Ghananians: distorted pronunciation of Ghanians Angolians: distorted pronunciation of Angolians.**

Congolians: distorted pronunciation of Congolese.

ABOUT THE AUTHOR

Jemadari Vi-Bee-Kil Kilele is a playwright and poet.
He is an educationist and a political activist.

So, grab a seat _____ you'll only need the edge.

20th May 2022

www.ingramcontent.com/pod-product-compliance
Lightning Source LLC
Chambersburg PA
CBHW071901070526
44583CB00016B/1785